PRIČA O BROJEVIMA

THE NUMBER STORY

SMALL BOOK ONE

ENGLISH - MONTENEGRIN

Numbers Teach Children
Their Number Names

written and illustrated by

MISS ANNA

Early Reader Edition of *The Number Story 1*
Bronze Medal Winner, 2016 Wishing Shelf Book Award

Library of Congress Control Number: 2018902040

Names: Miss Anna, author.
Title: Number story : numbers teach children their number names / Miss Anna.
Description: Portland, OR: Lumpy Publishing, 2018.
Identifiers: ISBN 978-1-945977-84-8 | LCCN 2018902040
Summary: The pictures and rhymes present stories which introduce numbers 0-10.
Subjects: LCSH Numeration—English--Montenegrin--Pictorial works--Juvenile literature. | BISAC JUVENILE NONFICTION /
Languages: English--Montenegrin
Classification: LCC QA141.3 .M57 2018 | DDC 513—dc23

Publisher: Lumpy Publishing
Website: www.missannabooks.com
Email: missanna@missannabooks.com

Paperback: ISBN 978-1-945977-84-8
Printed in the U.S.A.   1 3 5 7 9 10 8 6 4 2

Želite li da naučite
naše brojeve?

It is very easy and a lot of fun!

Lako i je zaista zanimljivo!

Say-along our little jingle

Hajde, pjevajte sa nama!

starting from Number One!

Krenimo sa brojem Jedan!

ONE looks like my one finger.

JEDAN

On je prav kao moj prst.

ONE!

JEDAN!

2

TWO   trails a tail.

DVA

On ima mali rep.

A TAIL! REP!

3

THREE has bumps.

TRI

On ima svoja brdašca.

Pogledajte njegova brdašca!

4

F O U R carries a sail.

ČETIRI

On ima jedro kao brod.

A SAIL!
Jedro kao brod!

5

FIVE   is a racing track.

PET

On je kao staza za trkanje.

VROOM
BRMM!
1

SIX   curves like a snail.

ŠEST

On migolji kao puž.

A SNAIL! PUŽ!

7

SEVEN has a sharp angle.

SEDAM

On ima oštar ugao.

BE CAREFUL! IT'S SHARP!

Pazi! Oštro!

8

E I G H T   is rollercoaster rails.

OSAM

On je kao tobogan.

JUHU!

YIPPEE!

NINE   is a bubble on a stick.

DEVET

On izgleda kao balon na štapu.

A BUBBLE!   BALON!

Izgleda kao kitovo oko.

MIG! MIG!
WINK!

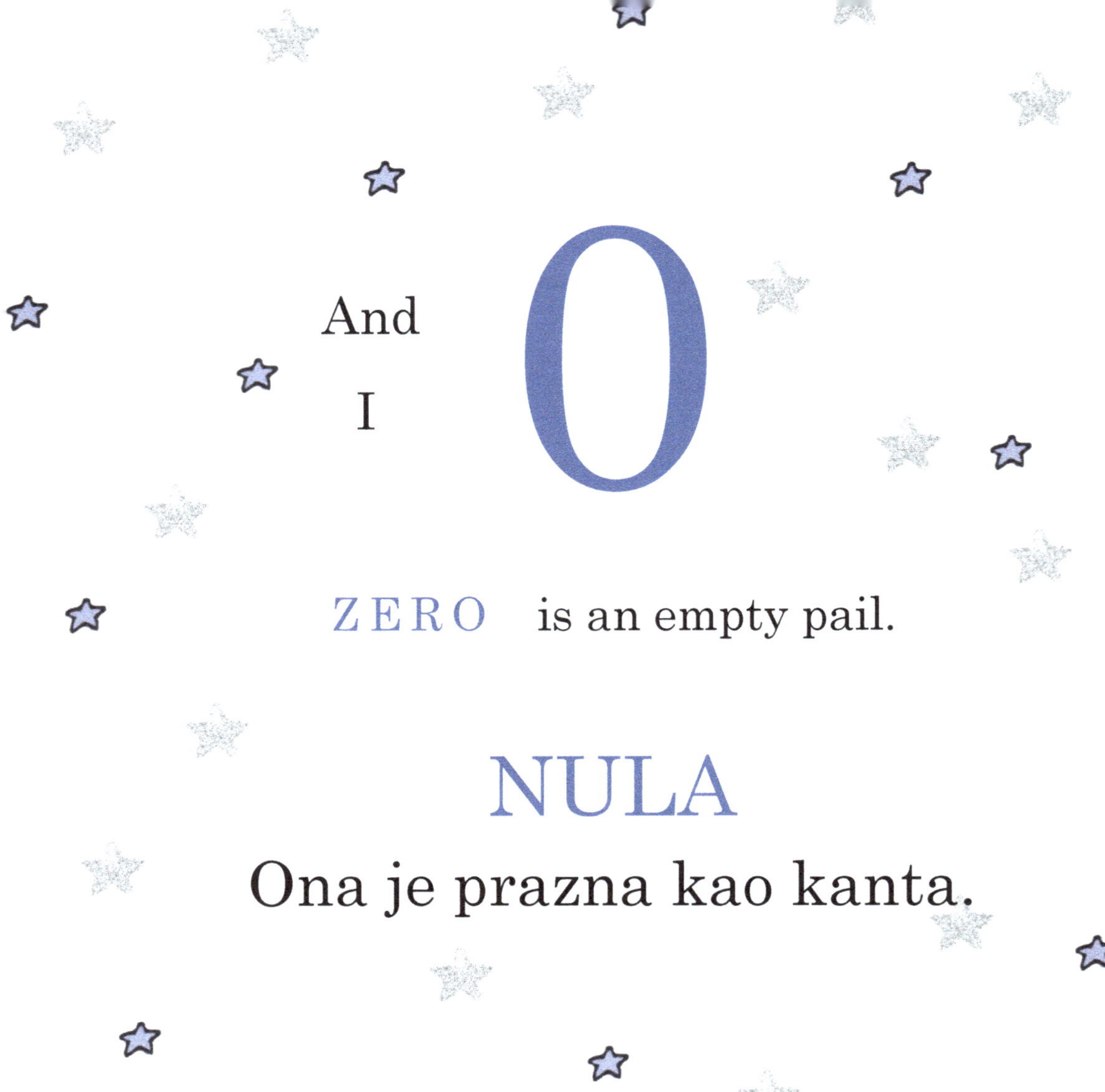

And I

0

ZERO   is an empty pail.

NULA

Ona je prazna kao kanta.

IT'S EMPTY!
Ništa, prazna!

Thank you for playing with us today.

We had a lot of fun too!

Hvala što ste se igrali sa nama.

I nama je bilo zanimljivo!

We are your Number friends,
Zero to Ten,
Who will be here for you~
Mi smo brojevi i tvoji smo drugari.
Mi smo uvijek uz tebe.

Bye-bye now!
See you again soon!
Doviđenja za sada!
Vidimo se opet!

The Numbers are *SINGING* too!

To sing-a-long, look for Miss Anna Number Story at your favorite music store like iTUNES.

MP3

Numbers 0-10
IDENTIFYING
& COUNTING

Numbers 11-20
& Ordinals
first, second, third...

Numbers 0-100
& Place Values
ones, tens, hundreds...

About Clocks
& Telling Time
hours, minutes, seconds...

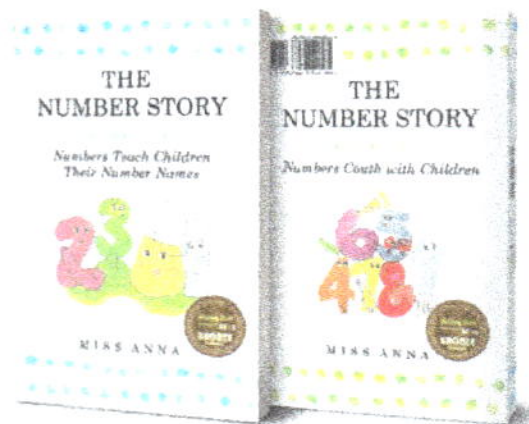

Number Story 1 & 2
isbn: 978-0-996216-48-7

Number Story 3 & 4
isbn: 978-1-945977-01-5

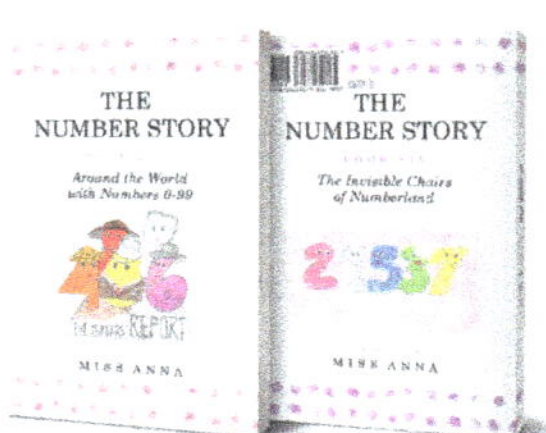

Number Story 5 & 6
isbn: 978-1-945977-06-0

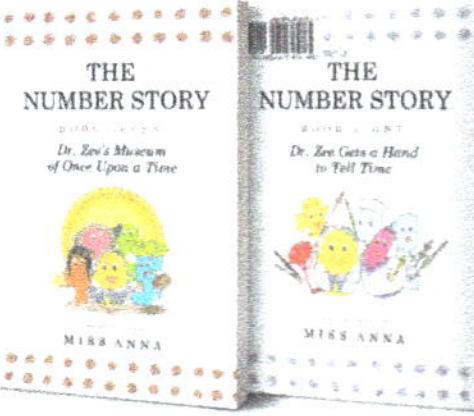

Number Story 7 & 8
isbn: 978-1-949320-40-4

For more Miss Anna books to love,
visit us at

www.missannabooks.com

Numbers are working hard all over the world!
Come Travel the World with Us!

www.ingramcontent.com/pod-product-compliance
Lightning Source LLC
Chambersburg PA
CBHW040859070726

47599CB00035B/2233